Dinosaur Detectives

Search for the Facts ...

Moschops
and Other Ancient Reptiles

Tracey Kelly

BROWN BEAR BOOKS

Published by Brown Bear Books Ltd

4877 N. Circulo Bujia
Tucson, AZ 85718
USA

and

Leroy House
436 Essex Rd
London N1 3QP
UK

ISBN 978-1-78121-404-6

Library of Congress Cataloging-in-Publication Data available on request

Text: Tracey Kelly
Designer: John Woolford
Design Manager: Keith Davis
Editorial Director: Lindsey Lowe
Children's Publisher: Anne O'Daly
Picture Manager: Sophie Mortimer

Picture Credits
Public Domain: Granger 4.

Brown Bear Books has made every attempt to contact the copyright holder.
If you have any information, please contact: licensing@brownbearbooks.co.uk

Manufactured in the United States of America

CPSIA compliance information: Batch#AG/5609

Websites
The website addresses in this book were valid at the time of going to press. However, it is possible that contents or addresses may change following publication of this book. No responsibility for any such changes can be accepted by the author or the publisher. Readers should be supervised when they access the Internet.

Contents

How Do We Know about Dinosaurs?

Scientists are like detectives.

They look at dinosaur fossils.

Fossils tell us where ancient reptiles lived.

They tell us how big they were.

Robert Broom was a dinosaur detective. He found *Moschops* fossils in 1910. He found them in South Africa. *Moschops* had a thick skull. People guessed that it used its head to fight.

How to Use This Book

This tells you what the animal ate.

🌿 Plant-eater

🦎 Meat-eater

These tell you when the animal lived.

260 million years ago

PERMIAN PERIOD

Moschops

(Say it!) (MOE-shops)

Moschops was a heavy animal.
Its legs were very strong.
It had blunt teeth. It ate plants.

How big am I?

13 ft (4 m)

Massive, heavy body

Strong legs

⚫ MINI FACTS
Moschops had a thick skull. It probably fought using its head.

16

FACT FILE
NAME: *Moschops* means "calf face"
WEIGHT: up to 660 pounds (300 kg)
FOOD: plants and bushes; may have eaten some meat
HABITAT: dry areas

Large jaws and blunt teeth

First found in South Africa, 1910

17

This shows you how big the animal was.

A map shows where the first fossils were found.

Read on to become a dinosaur detective!

What Was Earth Like?

Moschops lived in the Permian period.

That was millions of years ago.

Earth was very dry.

Plants grew near water pools.

Ancient reptiles ate and drank there.

Bradysaurus

Say it! (BRAY-dee-SAW-rus)

Bradysaurus had a huge body.
It had strong limbs. Its head had bony
ridges. Its teeth were shaped like leaves.

Head "crown" made
of bony ridges

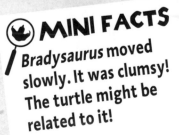

🔍 **MINI FACTS**

Bradysaurus moved
slowly. It was clumsy!
The turtle might be
related to it!

How big am I?

8 ft (2.5 m)

FACT FILE

NAME: *Bradysaurus* means "Brady's lizard" or "slow reptile"

WEIGHT: up to 1 ton (1 tonne)

FOOD: plants

HABITAT: large swamps

Big body

Hard scales

Short, strong limbs

First found in ...
South Africa, 1914

9

Coelurosauravus

Say it! (SEEL-your-oh-SAW-rave-us)

Coelurosauravus looked like a lizard with wings! Each wing had 22 tiny bones. These were covered with skin. *Coelurosauravus* could glide in the air.

How big am I?

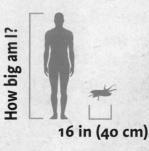

16 in (40 cm)

MINI FACTS

Coelurosauravus was the first animal that could glide.

Long head with frill

Long tail
helped flight

FACT FILE

NAME: *Coelurosauravus* means
"hollow-tipped reptile bird"

WEIGHT: about 1 pound (0.5 kg)

FOOD: insects in the trees

HABITAT: woodland
in Germany, England,
and Madagascar

Lizardlike legs

Wings opened
like a fan

First found in ...
Madagascar, 1926

Dicynodon

Say it! (dye-SINE-oh-don)

Dicynodon looked like a pig!

It had a bulky body, It had strong legs.

Its large teeth could break off plants.

Horny beak, used
to bite plants

FACT FILE

NAME: *Dicynodon* means "two dog-teeth"

WEIGHT: 24 pounds (11 kg)

FOOD: plants and roots

HABITAT: most lived on land, but a few lived in the water.

How big am I?

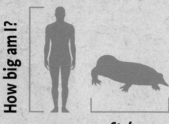

4 ft (1.2 m)

Piglike body shape

MINI FACTS

Dicynodon lived in groups. This kept it safe from meat-eaters.

Short tail

First found in ...
South Africa, 1845

13

Dimetrodon

Say it! (dye-MEE-troe-don)

Dimetrodon had a huge head.

It had a "sail" of skin on its back.

The sail soaked up the sun's heat.

Sharp teeth for cutting meat

🔍 MINI FACTS

Dimetrodon had long teeth for tearing flesh. It had short teeth for chewing.

Skin like a reptile's

How big am I?

11 ft (3.5 m)

Sail of skin

FACT FILE

NAME: *Dimetrodon* means "two measures of teeth"

WEIGHT: 550 pounds (250 kg)

FOOD: animals and insects

HABITAT: swamps of the southwestern United States, Canada, Russia, and Eastern Europe

First found in ...
Texas and Oklahoma, 1870s

Legs spread out
to the sides

Moschops

Say it! (MOE-shops)

Moschops was a heavy animal.
Its legs were very strong.
It had blunt teeth. It ate plants.

How big am I?

13 ft (4 m)

Massive, heavy body

Strong legs

🔍 MINI FACTS

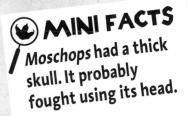

Moschops had a thick skull. It probably fought using its head.

FACT FILE

NAME: *Moschops* means "calf face"

WEIGHT: up to 660 pounds (300 kg)

FOOD: plants and bushes; may have eaten some meat

HABITAT: dry areas

Large jaws and blunt teeth

First found in ...
South Africa, 1910

17

Lystrosaurus

Say it! (LISS-tro-SAW-russ)

Lystrosaurus had wide feet.

They helped it walk on swampy ground.

Some reptiles lived in the Triassic period.

☀ MINI FACTS

Lystrosaurus probably lived in or near water. It lived in herds. That kept it safe.

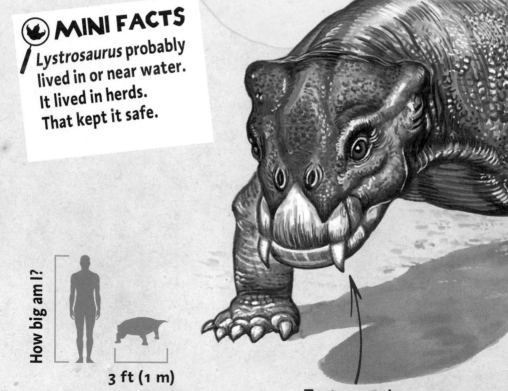

How big am I?

3 ft (1 m)

Tusks, used to tear plants

FACT FILE

NAME: *Lystrosaurus* means "shovel lizard"

WEIGHT: 200 pounds (91 kg)

FOOD: water plants

HABITAT: near swamps, lakes, and coasts around the world

Heavy, barrel-shaped body

Short, stubby tail

First found in ...
South Africa, 1867

19

Euparkeria

💬 Say it! (YOU-park-EAR-ree-ah)

Euparkeria had a tiny body.

It had long back legs.

It ran fast to hunt prey.

How big am I?

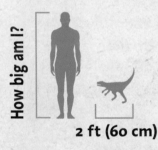

2 ft (60 cm)

🐦 **MINI FACTS**

Euparkeria could run very fast. It could probably run across water and not fall in!

Sharp teeth, used to kill prey

Long tail, used for balance

FACT FILE

NAME: *Euparkeria* means "Parker's reptile"

WEIGHT: up to 10 pounds (4.5 kg)

FOOD: smaller animals

HABITAT: forest floors in the woodlands of South Africa

Ran on two legs

First found in ...
South Africa, 1913

21

Dinosaur Quiz

Test your dinosaur detective skills!
Can you answer these questions?
Look in the book for clues.
The answers are on page 24.

1 What kind of teeth did *Bradysaurus* have? What did it eat?

2 Which dinosaur lived near swamps, lakes, and coasts?

3 Why did *Dimetrodon* have a sail on its back?

4 Was *Euparkeria* a fast or slow runner?

Glossary

fossil
Part of an animal or plant in rock.
The animal or plant lived in ancient times.

habitat
The kind of place where an animal usually lives.

herd
A group of animals that lives together.

meat-eater
An animal that eats mostly meat.

plant-eater
An animal that eats only plants.

prey
An animal that is hunted
by other animals for food.

Triassic period
The time that
came after the
Permian period.

Find out More

Books

National Geographic Little Kids First Big Book of Dinosaurs, Catherine D. Hughes (National Geographic Kids, 2011)

The Big Book of Dinosaurs, DK Editors (DK Children, 2015)

Websites

discoverykids.com/category/dinosaurs/

www.kidsdinos.com

www.ngkids.co.uk/games/dinosaurCove

Index

Quiz Answers: 1. *Bradysaurus* had leaf-shaped teeth. It ate plants.
2. *Lystrosaurus.* **3.** The sail helped *Dimetrodon* soak up heat from the sun.
4. It was a fast runner.